Gallery Books
Editor: Peter Fallon

TIME AND THE ISLAND

Seán Dunne

TIME
AND THE
ISLAND

Gallery Books

Time and the Island
is first published
simultaneously in paperback
and in a clothbound edition
on 29 February 1996.

The Gallery Press
Loughcrew
Oldcastle
County Meath
Ireland

ISBN 1 85235 180 2 (*paperback*)
    1 85235 181 0 (*clothbound*)

The Gallery Press receives financial assistance from An Chomhairle
Ealaíon / The Arts Council, Ireland.

Contents

for Trish Edelstein

A man past forty
May flourish like a tree
But a grave opened
Changes his face.

— after the Welsh

'It isn't that one brings life together — it's that one will not allow it to be torn apart.'
— Muriel Rukeyser

Letter to Lisbon

All night I was alone.
I heard only the sound
Of a convent bell at dawn,
The syllables of your name
In each peal and its aftermath.

I float on the river
Of what happens:
A boat adrift
When the rudder's lost.
You are with me. Riverbanks beckon.

To touch your sleeve now
Would just be enough.
Even that would be better
Than the long night ahead
Knowing you will not call.

If I were a leaf loosened
From a tree near your room
I would float to your sill
And wait for you to take me
To mark the last page you read.

෴

I have given up doubt,
That old, worn-out coat.
All that's constant
Is the fact of change:
Pearl of love, grit of pain.

෴

My room warms my work:
The deep fire reddening.
Yet nothing touches me
Like the heat of your hand
Against my closed eyelids.

෴

One day you linked arms
And my arm tingles still
As if even through winter coats
Touch traces the line
That led us to each other.

෴

Moorhens close their wings.
Cats curl near the fireguard.
My children huddle and sigh.
With the fact of your absence,
Am I the only one awake in the world?

I think of you asleep.
I want to reach across Europe
To trace your hair and stroke
Your face as I would a child's,
Your breath warm wool on my fingers.

Once I flicked a crumb
From your skirt in a restaurant.
What lies I make my hands tell:
What could I care for crumbs?
It was you I wanted to touch.

In wild moments I wonder
Would I be better as a bullfrog
From some Japanese poem,
Wet and croaking at your feet,
Offering my song like a handsel?

Light which has no feeling
Can reach you through a chink.
Mirrors can hold your face;
Dead walls know your touch.
Yet I who want you must do without.

～

I look at the hand you held.
It flops and seems inert,
(So plain with long fingers,
The nails I barely bite)
But for the memory of your hand.

～

Cold rooms of your girlhood,
Dull lanes of Macclesfield.
Closed streets of my boyhood,
Coums and lakes of Waterford.
As if at the Equator, they meet in our talk.

～

I hear a blackbird's call
In the mist each morning.
I say your name as if sound
Might stretch across space
Like the bird's clear song.

～

Your shells line a sill.
I hold one to my ear
And hear the sea heaving,
Its slow, repetitive rhythm
A lesson in patience I must learn.

I walk on a cliff and count
The lights of fishing-boats:
Fireflies on a dark sea.
Such lights are our days together.
Around them, absence darkens.

Happiness

after Akhmatova

These are the days before spring:
The meadow at ease under piled snow,
The dry leaves rustling with pleasure,
The wind warm, tender and supple,
And the body delights in its lightness,
And you can't even tell your own house,
And the song that once drove you mad
You sing now with rapture, as if it were new.

Wishing for the Border

I want to sit with you in a warm kitchen.
Outside it is raining. Steam rises

From our clothes on the silver bar
Of the range where a kettle heats.

On the table a knife, chunks
Of bread baked this morning.

You go to your room and change.
Through the door, I hear that song —

The one you sang an hour ago
Before we kissed on a road in rain

Lit by the glare of cars
Panning us: searchlights in a camp.

I eat and watch you comb red hair,
Your head aslant before a mirror.

Now let us lie closer than refugees,
Our lips touching in the attic dark

While around us the landscape is still
As a held breath, the only sound

A dog barking across fields —
A farmyard animal, or a border guard's.

Still Lives

Shells and dried flowers,
A row of antique bottles
(Phials from a closed pharmacy,
Powder hardened on glass)
And light through a skylight
In annunciation.

❧

The still life of your corner —
A half-read book, stray
Strands of hair in a brush,
Ampoules of soap and a torn
Envelope near a nightdress:
All of it framed with your presence.

❧

Torch songs in an empty room.
With you gone, who can I tell
Of that slow descending note
Or that phrase where a voice cracks
And quivers with heartbreak?
I save it like news for your return.

❧

The scraps of a life together —
Tree-houses in a child's drawing,
Crumbs on a chipped breadboard,
Herbs bundled near a cookbook,
Autumn stripping a sapling's leaves —
I never notice when you are here.

Your smell stays in the sheets.
I lie on your side of the bed
And inhale our last love-making,
The memory opening like a cave
Towards which I swell and surge
As your lost cries mingle with bells.

I wake in the night and turn
To the cold that takes your place.
Above our skylight the stars
Make shapes that shine on you
In a far country. Among them, the moon
Grants us equal light.

One Sunday in the Gearagh

In the long grass of the Gearagh
   You stretch and sleep
      Your head at an angle to my head

A moth flits
   And hovers above you
      Makes a light brooch in your hair

Cows mooch in damp fields
   Lazy heads lifted
      When we pass on thin paths

Stumps of trees around us
   A drowned forest and a drowned
      Village called Annahala

Lichen on trees, moss on stones,
   Sparrows — nifty commas —
      Dart on the sky's wide page

I tell you of the man who rowed
   Across the waters to his house
      And drowned on his way home

Afternoon of perfume
   Flowers crushed beneath feet
      Scents yielded like secrets

Bog-cotton in a meadow
    Lighter than your hair
        Your fingers lighter than leaves

Your face smooth against mine
    A slim wind between us
        The ghost of an old argument

Scanning the lake for otters
    We settle for paired swans
        White porcelain among reeds

Islands stud the waters
    Legions of the drowned
        Raising their torn heads

Meadows shimmer with movement
    Tortoise-shell and meadow-brown
        Butterflies in a haze of heat

I stroke your closed eyes
    And kiss the lids. I nudge
        The tip of each light lash.

Oak stumps everywhere
    Suppurating wounds
        The black days we have known

A heron stands
    Sentry over water
        Curled initial on vellum

As we cross old quarry roads
Hands linked like branches
Of rose-trees in a ballad

Three Love Poems

after Paul Eluard

The Woman in Love

She stands on my eyelids
And her hair is in mine.
She has my hands' shape
And the colour of my eyes.
She is swallowed in my shadow
Like a stone beneath the sky.

Her eyes forever open
And she will not let me sleep.
Her dreams make suns evaporate
In the broad light of day,
Make me laugh, cry and laugh,
Even when there's nothing to say.

No One Can Know Me

No one can know me better
Than you have known me

Your eyes in which we sleep
Both together
Make for my man's glare
A fate better than any made for the world's night

Your eyes in which I voyage
Give to road-signs a meaning
Detached from the earth

In your eyes all those who reveal
Our infinite solitude
Are no longer what they thought

No one can know you
Better than I know you

At the Window

My brow against the panes
Nightwatchmen of sorrow
Sky with darkness I surpass
Plains tiny in my open hands
Inert indifferent
My brow against the panes
Nightwatchmen of sorrow
I seek you without hope
Way beyond myself
And I love you so much
I can no longer tell which of us is absent.

The Butterfly Soul

Butterflies freed
From nets at a wine-party
    Circle and fly

To the fairest
There, landing on hair
    With poised wings:

Spirits of emperors,
Souls of ancestors, lost
    Lovers in a daze.

As if in a world
Without enmity, they trust
    Tanks, guns, glint

Of a bayonet's edge,
Or a soldier's corpse,
    His spirit fled

And fluttering
On a finger at the Somme,
    Trembling at a nail.

A fallen flower
Searching for a branch, it
    Floats in silence.

A man dreamed
He was a butterfly, then woke
In a wingless world

Wishing for flight
To a bamboo room, keeping
A promise in love

Like the butterfly
Landing on a hairpin to choose
An emperor's wife

Or another who flew
To a cemetery set with flowers,
Wings cracked with grief.

On the edge of lush
Cabbages one flutters, set
Like a brooch on a coat —

A soul in flight
Above my writing-table,
Perched on the edge

Of my paper space,
An ancestor's visit
Landing in a furious

Flutter near my hand:
Silent applause or reproof
For powdered palms —

As a child I killed
One, its death in the garden
    A catastrophe of wings,

    Broken sails adrift,
Its body ripped, while I waited
    Wishing for flight

    To absolve the act
Learning that cruelty, pain
    Wait in a chrysalis

    Then hover and alight
On lives, our wings too frail
    Against such weather.

The Art of Tea

Leaves

Let them be creased
Like a horseman's boot,
Curled like the dewlap
Of a bullock.
Let them unfold
Like mist in a ravine,
Turn wet and soft
Like earth rinsed with rain.

Cup

The blue glaze
Of southern jade:
The perfect hollow
Of a teacup.

Stir with
A bamboo whisk.
Drink and feel
The soul flood.

Boiling

Bubbles begin:
the eyes of fishes.
Bubbles swell:
crystals in a pool.
Bubbles burst:
waves in a storm.

Tea-room

Let it be solitary
as a cottage on a beach.
Let no sword sully
this abode of vacancy.
With linen napkin
and bamboo dipper,
let it be a shrine
for the ordinary,
for talk of tea
and the taking of tea,
best made with water
from a mountain spring.

A Shrine for Lafcadio Hearne,
1850-1904

Like an artist painting on rice-grains,
He tried to trap Japan in a story:
His one good eye so close to the page
He might have been a jeweller with a gem.

So much to tell: kimonos and cranes,
Cemeteries to stalk at evening, slow
Shoals of candles — souls
On rivers beneath a massive moon.

Even the sound of sandals on a bridge
Stayed in the mind for an evening,
Matching the shadow of fishermen
On still waters: a painted print.

Or a face smiling to hide its grief,
The touch of passing sleeves
Part of a plan that maps the future,
A heron seeking the heights on a wall.

Loneliness ended in Matsue: that raw
Pain no longer gnawing like the Creole
Songs on a sidewalk in New Orleans.
Instead he heard a flute's clear note.

He was a lantern drifting from the shore,
Dissolving in the tone of a struck bell.
Sipping green tea in Tokyo, he heard
Ghost stories from an impossible past

And died past fifty from his Western heart.
Afterwards, he was a story still told, set
Firmly as rocks in a Zen garden.
Incense burns near cake at his shrine.

In the sound of sandals on a bridge
I hear him sometimes, or catch him
In the swift calligraphy of a scroll,
Or in the curve of a rough bowl.

A breeze through a bamboo-grove,
His memory passes for an instant.
Snow falls on his grave and on plum-blossom.
He is fading like a fisherman in mist.

Shiatsu Sequence

Shoes

As if before a temple,
I leave my shoes outside:
Clutter in a corner,
Cares that I discard.

The Mat

I press my face against it,
Its smell of herbs and oil:
A pattern rich with potions,
Stories it's absorbed.

Chimes

Cylinders wait for the wind
To claim their metal song.
Watching them, I wait for you
To free hurt like a bird.

Knots

Muscles ease at your touch,
Nets of knots you discover.
You work until they open:
A mother loosening laces.

Tears

Tears pour as if a prophet
Tapped a rock with a stick.
You draw them out: threads
To twist in comfort's rug.

Oil

Its smell fills the room,
A rattle of jars and bowls.
The sound of it pouring:
Milk from tiny teats.

Scarf

A heron flashes from reeds
And grips the fish in a pool.
It is over: your peace a scarf
In which my cares lie bundled.

Matching the Note

A piano tinkles as a cradle rocks,
A lullaby tapped in tuned morse
When a blackbird stops at a window,
Adding to the song its own sound.
It pecks at berries and then,
As if to match the ivory note,
Resumes its music on the sill
In a world where wishes seem granted.

Russians in Paris

1

When cities crumbled before the Reds
And houses were broken by hordes
(Double bedrooms now to sleep twelve,
Library shelves axed for firewood),
They slid across Europe in trains,
Huddled in fur, with the soft
Faces of frightened animals.
History was a hopeless arrogance
Where postmen became commissars,
The summerhouse an office
Where former serfs ruled
Over a future blacker than caviar.

2

In Paris life went on and breath
Seldom froze in the winter air.
Children rolled hoops on lawns
And wives shopped on boulevards
That, at a stretch, matched Moscow.
At home with chants of bearded priests,
Incense rose before icons smuggled
With roubles, silver, a loved toy.
The Seine was no Volga but still
It beat the bottom of a stream

Or a grave in gardens where once
The seasons seemed made by moods.
Their sleeping daughters looked
Lost daughters of the murdered tsar.

3

The shop on the Mont de Ste Geneviève
Is a gloomy dacha on the hill's slope.
Among icons and toys, stacks
Of books and pictures of patriarchs,
I saw two posters of poets on a wall.
One died in a camp, his poems kept
By a wife who absorbed them like food.
Another knew how poems could draw
Black Marias at the heart of night.
I know her poems like prayers,
Their words clustered berries
On a branch to which I hold.
When I ask the poster's price
I am told: *She is not for sale.*

4

Violins on steps of the church,
Petals over furred heads.
Funeral of the film-maker,
Funeral of the dancer whose eyes
Loomed from Calvary at the end.
Flowers teem in a cemetery
Bright with resurrection.

The dancer was a wounded faun,
A face full of age and answers.
His coffin moved through Paris
Like music through the memory
As all of them move now
Across steppes of time in snow.

The Lesson

Toy boats in the Luxembourg Gardens
Circle small oceans to the roar
Of children engrossed in the lesson
Of life as an abandoned shore.

Heading for Crete

i.m. Claire Barker

Did you ever think you'd see the day
I'd write a poem with your name
And *in memoriam* at the head of it?

When I called to you in hospital
Your skin was a worn parchment,
Worry-lines quilled around your eyes

As you curled to meet the pain's demand.
My every word came out so bland
While you, withered in a white

Cardigan, a drip fang in your wrist,
Watched a mirror and palmed into place
Your hair that thinned with therapy.

Your room was a storm of flowers in bowls.
You slipped in and out of sleep's lair,
Fingers searching for water or a comb.

Claire, you had more pillows than the princess
In the tale had mattresses over the pea,
And still you too felt the hard pain start.

You said when this was over you were going
To Crete, to bask among islands and ruined
Palaces in the Mediterranean sun.

Beside you, fruit was piled in bowls
With wholefood bars, nuts and grapes,
As if by taking all that's perfect

You could blunt the pincer's edge.
Before leaving I kissed you and your lips
Were powdery moth-wings. Years on,

I think of that touch and of you in Crete,
The sea glinting like a raised axe
And your arm waving as the tide turns.

A Leaf in *The Aeneid*

for Ellen Beardsley

In your copy of *The Aeneid*, there's
A leaf pressed between pages.
Its stem stiff and dry, it marks

The wooden horse of Troy, a belly
Heavy with death in a Greek gift.
Veins twist through the leaf like tales

Spun around a winter fire.
It lasts with language handed down
As I hand this gift to you who love

And have learned to trust horses,
Who found in firm mane and swivelling eye
Trust without treachery, no hiding hurt.

Five Photographs by
Thomas Merton

The observed particulars take on the mystery of revelation . . .

The Hermitage

A house for quiet built in the woods,
One good place for a man alone.
Trees surround it and jets fly over
Halfway through a psalm, words caught
In the slipstream and blown away.
It sits within the lens and seems
A shack for solitude in the wide world.

Still Life

A chair, a ladder, a bowl, wood
Strewn with shavings on a plain floor.
Behind the chair, an old cup stained
With rainwater. Singled within
The frame he fixed, they are firm
And plain, mundane as the shadow
Of chair on bowl, ladder-rung on chair.

The Broom

The broom in a corner remains
No more than a broom, its bristles
Firm when fingers press,

Its handle smooth from months of use.
There are no messages here; no moral lurks
In the plain wall or the bunched broom.
Take it or leave it. It swishes and sweeps.

Icons

From a distance, they might be framed
Pictures of high-school friendships,
Students with scrolls and gowns,
Family portraits in studios.
Closer, a worn madonna pines
On painted wood. Near her, the flecked
Faces of prophets stare.

Writing Table

Words spilt despite the silence,
A curved lamp over them as they formed
In spiral notebooks. So little
To say for it: its sheaves of paper,
Its marked book and pair of pens.
All it lacks is a mouse from Kells,
Perched on a word while the monk sleeps.

Simone Weil, 1909-1940

A mind enclosed in language is in prison . . .

I have come to love you in photographs,
Your thin face never yielding to ease
And your coat about you like a cape
Gathered against the cold of quaysides.
I passed your old school near the Pantheon
And imagined you among children walking
Near pillars pocked with bullet-holes.

You would have spent your life before
Leonardo's *Last Supper*, lured by lines
That draw you always to Christ's face.
You limped around Italy in the peace
Of paintings and darkened chapels
But I think of you most in France,
An abbey at evening as chant soars

And settles in a shawl of silence.
You spread books across the floor
And peered as if words were ants
Teeming on the page as in a crack
Where meaning, like light, might fall.
When you died starving, waiting on God,
No realm of words could call you back.

Sisters

Martha

Her mind a packed picnic basket,
A woman so busy she calls
Boys by brothers' names and longs
For hours alone in olive groves.
Her dreamy sister hunkers near the low-
Voiced visitor whose talk she'd follow
If goats were gathered and basil plucked.

Mary

To sit in silence and listen
As pots chortle and oil in urns
Warms near a sunlit doorway —
An act more simple than frisking
Crumbs from aprons, or arching
A fine finger in trails of dust:
And yet like this to enter history.

The Petition

Grey Gobnait stands above a lone
Woman kneeling in grass near a well.
Cattle slouch over acres
Carrying their own weight like weights
Of the world on the woman's mind.
She tightens her scarf and prays.

Cold water from the well,
The plastic cup cracked and peeling.
Like a cloak on the saint's shoulders
Quiet settles on the evening.
On a heavy stick, the woman walks
Towards Ballyvourney and Ballymakeera.

The Egg Collector

In a dark corner of the rectory, he placed eggs in rows in a mahogany case. Some were slightly cracked as if taken while swollen with birth. He thought of the firm life inside, unhatched and hopeless: a song stopped in a throat. His daughter painted watercolours in another room and, by the fire in the drawing-room, his wife worked at silhouettes. He consulted his egg books, loving the clear plates of the Reverend Morris. Each egg seemed suspended in space: a plain or speckled planet floating in the clear sky of the page. The thought of Mr Darwin darted through his mind but he banished it like a cobweb. Golden eagle. Crow. Black-headed Bunting. Chaffinch. Sedge Warbler. Lesser Whitethroat. Specimens sent from Oxford rooms. Tomorrow, a parcel would arrive bearing, packed in straw, the egg of the Grey Plover, sent by the Reverend Tristram in Durham. He trembled at the thought, holding the pale egg of a kingfisher in his hands as if his palms that earlier rested on the wide pages of a Bible had now become interlaced nests.

From his window, he saw moonlight fall on headstones: so many he had seen buried, his black stole flapping in the breeze over delicate girls and bearded patriarchs. He held an egg high and surveyed the sky behind it, the shell a focus for all that was frail. His daughter's laughter reached him. He closed the lid on the case and imagined the chirps of birds pleading to be released. He shoved the thought aside. So much was hardly worth thinking about. Others could make the century tremble and crack and roll. Tomorrow his parcel will arrive and his hands will part the rustling straw.

Three Women in January

A January evening of imminent snow.
I pace my garden and search
Gaps in hedges as if to know
Some space where answers fall to earth.
Clothes in the machine spin round
And smog smothers the stars that fail
To pierce the city's weight of soot.
Taut grass crunches beneath my boots.

The night reminds of an absent friend,
Asleep near a fallen book or now
Awake to soothe a restless child
Who'll wake to whistle with birds.
Her cottage faces a road of ghosts.
In the garden a swing is still.
Near her, a plant stirs on a sill
As if sensing a snowflake's fall.

The scent of crushed rosemary brings
Another to mind as the first flakes float,
Her dark hair curled and her hands
Deft as a lacemaker's when she draws
Patterns in space to declare a point.
Things that summon her I can quote —
Gusts that graze like an angel's wing,
The wooden button of a duffel-coat.

In my slanted attic another sleeps
Whose touch I sense, whose trust I keep.
Snow falls fast and blurs the fine
Cloth of her blouse on the stiff line.
Buds thicken on the tree she planted,
Its bare branches no more than strokes.
The curve she makes when fast asleep
I'll curl towards later, a shape complete.

Light from windows frames the edged
Tracery of hedges frosted with webs.
Drops freeze and dangle from threads.
The machine goes still, a sudden death.
Cats cry out among the yards
And moonlight breaks the wall of smog,
That sight a blessing now that spills
On women, friendship, the filled hedges.

Francis Ledwidge's Cottage

I remember his small poems, country
Intimacies in fading ink;
An old fiddle, books, a small
Virgin set in a shell from the Front.
In the garden, bees seemed from a page.

It became the measure of what followed,
A day of devoured happiness,
Our breaths in the dark of tumuli
Crossing in a single cloud.
Nothing again could ever live up to it.

In a photograph we stand at the door,
Your hair in the wind, my beard that's shaved.
We could be some couple looking for roots
At the homestead where it all began,
Heady with achievement of a moment's grace.

Time and the Island

for Diarmuid Ó Drisceoil

The Pact

When she left the island and married
Into Schull, she made her husband swear
To bury her on Cape when the time came.
When she died, boats carried
Her corpse beneath cliffs and sailed
In the shape of a cross on the open sea
With her bright coffin at its core,
And her husband near it to guide her home.

Ashes

In the weeks before he died, the old
Storyteller whose talk became books
Ripped pages, rooted out poems
From cupboards, boxes, dressers and tins.
He burned them in a barrel out the back
As cancer gathered inside him and wore
Away all that saw worth in words.
Ashes flecked his face as the blaze roared.

Lough Ioral

Near the lake with magic waters, I walk
Over washerwomen's flat stones. As if
For a stiff-collared photographer, ghosts

Pose as petticoats are stretched
And slapped with a fury that blends
With cross-talk in a sepia morning.
I move among them and their words
That time tore: threads from a hem.

Walls

Sunlight spills between grey
Walls that snake through fields.
A stone shifts from a place it kept
For centuries and disturbs
The rhythm of a wall that shivers slightly.
Windmills wave their frantic arms.
Coves cry against the push of breakers.
Tokens of lost time, small flowers break through.

The Old Church

Sheltering from rain in the saint's church,
I trace the line of lintel and sill.
Through thin windows, sermons distil
Meanings that make the moment change.
Headstones lean in the grass where wet
Scythes curve until the downpour stops.
Behind me, a generator hums with the drone
Of monks at Compline on a winter evening.

Car Door

A car door blocks a gap in a field.
Through its glassless window,
I watch the grass where a black goat stands
To look at the wind only goats can see.
The door frames an inner world.
Rust flecks its handle, the gleam gone from it.
Easy at last, I measure fields in light
That falls with forgiveness everywhere.

The Argument

1

I face again the disappointment
Of things pushed from their proper place:
The dry flowers in an old basket,
The photograph of a poet's home,
The eggs carved from cherry wood
And set in a bowl near the door,
The smell of you on a damp towel.
It all comes down in the end to these.

2

I would sing this if it had an air,
A theme I know from other times.
Hurt becomes habit and I reach
For rhetoric, the steel phrase,
But end with hands against my face
Rocking in silence as you turn your head,
Continents away in the same bed.

3

I want to walk with you in Bohernabreena
In the cold days after Christmas when dogs
Yap towards weirs and the stiff trees
Are iced with frost. It is years ago
And before us the future flows like smooth
Water falling with the semblance of silk.

4

A brief moon above a country road.
A song heard once on a late-night channel.
Blackberries uneaten in a narrow lane.

Separation

after Akhmatova

The evening path
Slopes before me.
Only yesterday, we were in love.
He begged me not to forget him.
Now there are only winds
And herdsmen calling,
And the clamour of cedars
By clear streams.

The Healing Island

My baggage rests on the quayside:
Warm clothes for a week of winds,
Notebooks for words that twitch
Like a stick gripped above water.

∽

A pyramid of turf in the grate.
Sparks spit and flutter in a chimney
Wide enough to inhale my cares,
Hoovering them with a fierce *whoosh*.

∽

Mountains on the mainland fade
As rain-clouds settle and swell.
Twelve summits disappear,
Apostles assumed into skies and stars.

∽

Silence in a children's burial ground.
I stop among souls that have not been
Hearing on wires a message from Limbo.
Stones are scattered like broken toys.

∽

I am missing you and long to tell
Of fissures in cracked stone,
Dragonflies on a well's skin,
Filaments where prisms form.

∾

To pass you with your red hair
Would draw bad luck to a boat.
Sooner turn back than risk such loss
Though mackerel teem in a sunlit sea.

∾

There is news of a corncrake heard
Among fields at the island's edge.
The story spreads in shops and lanes,
A hectic rumour of salvation.

∾

Night is closing like a claw
On islands where monks prayed.
Across hillsides pocked with warrens
Gusts gather the gist of psalms.

∾

Woken by roosters, I reach
For my one book and find it dull.
No page seems equal to the deep
Implosions of waves in coves.

∾

Minnows dart across pools
Quicker than thoughts in my head.
I crave the stillness of water:
Depths clear and surface sure.

&

Striations on stones, the worn
Force of centuries and the sea.
The thought of you as I work:
A glacier shifting earth's shape.

&

Smell of turf-smoke on island paths,
Stink of crab-claws in a ditch.
Reek of oil in a trawler's hold,
Odour of wax in a Sunday chapel.

&

Flowers teem on ditch and wall.
Packed as mussels, firm petals part.
Frail stems teach the most:
Thin as tissue, they outlast gales.

&

In a dream our hands meet,
Fingers splayed starfish.
Your cries rise with the cries
Of kittiwakes on sheer cliffs.

&

How to crack the cotton code
Of sheets billowing on lines?
From the pier they seem a signal
Inviting love to the far homes.

❧

An empty school faces the sea,
Models askew in windows:
Plasticine huts in a chalk quiet,
A playground empty of cries.

❧

I phone you from a call-box,
Windows misted and scratched.
Tones sound in an empty house,
A fact more bleak than gull's call.

❧

Columns of geese straddle the road.
The erect leader turns left,
Leading his squadron to rock-pools
Where they drink: sentries at ease.

❧

Sheared sheep tremble in folds,
Shreds of fleece catch in barbs.
Nets rot in an outhouse.
Hens lay in a rusted car.

❧

Wisps of bog-cotton on a hill,
Wisps of wool near a saint's well,
Wisps of smoke from a chimney:
Wisps of words to weave new ways.

༄

I remember being with you here:
Red hair against white sand,
Your black swimsuit among waves
Striking as a glimpsed seal.

༄

Neighbours' gifts: a creel of turf,
White eggs in a cardboard box,
A saucepan of cooked claws,
Mackerel wet from the bay.

༄

I gather shells from Duach beach.
Tiny as worries, they fill my palms.
The sea gives and neighbours give:
I open and yield to kindness.

༄

Let me cradle your head with my arm
And whisper love-poems, secrets.
Your hands in mine are loved.
Mine in yours are held in turn.

༄

Before leaving, I climb the mountain.
High among sheep and bladed winds,
I add my stone to the peak's cairn
And another for you: a summit reached.